Elephant Kids Color

+Fun Facts for Kids to Read about Elephants

Children Activity Book for Girls & Boys Age 4-8, with 30 Super Fun Coloring
Pages of Elephants in Lots of Fun Actions!

You can easily beat an elephant in a hide-n-seek game because the elephant is the largest animal on land! No more hiding!

Although the word "mammoth" means "huge", these woolly prehistoric elephants were actually about the size of an African elephant nowadays.

The mammoth's body was covered with 30–90 cm long guard hairs. These hairs did protect them from the harshly cold weather during the Ice Age.

Guess what animals the elephants are scared of? Probably none. You are wrong! Ants and bees are an elephant's greatest fears! Elephants fear that these small animals might get inside their trunks which of course are highly sensitive.

Handshaking is no way to greet an elephant! Elephant have their own ways of greeting. For instance, when two elephants meet each other, they often extend each other's trunks to welcome.

Don't worry, your friend elephant will never forget your face no matter how many people it meets. Elephants have great memory and recalling ability.

Where did that noise come from? Ask an elephant! Elephants are wonderful listeners and can hear sound waves reaching far beyond the human hearing range.

Ever wondered what might happen if elephants jumped? Yes, the whole earth would tremble down! There is only one mammal that cannot jump and it is the elephant.

Bedtimes are always fun but elephants do not think so. Wild elephants are only known to sleep for just 2 or 3 hours a day while at other times they travel long distances away from their predators.

A gift for an elephant? A pair of glasses! Scientists say that elephants are poor at eyesight but are excellent smellers!

Tusks, although attractive, can lead to an elephant's death! Elephant tusks have a substance called ivory which is believed to be of great value. Elephants are killed in mass by humans to steal this ivory. That definitely is a sad truth.

What makes the elephant extra-ordinary is its tusks. Did you know that elephant tusks are incisors that we normally have? They are mostly used to dig for water, roots, to debark trees and even to fight.

Elephants waive their trunks side to side and sometimes it almost looks like it is dancing! But remember, elephants do this to smell their surroundings better.

Rather than ears, elephants hear way better through their feet! Elephants can hear rumblings made by other elephants through the vibrations on the ground.

Saw a lone elephant? That is probably a male elephant since female elephants often travel in herds led by the oldest female called the 'matriarch' while the males tend to be wanderers.

What do you think is the elephant's most important limb? That's right, the trunk! The trunk is used for drinking water and is strong enough to shovel you right from the ground and sensitive enough to pick even the smallest blade of grass!

Looking from afar, you'd say all elephants are the same. But in fact, there are specifically three species of elephants in the world: the African forest elephant, the African savannah elephant, and the Asian elephant.

Oh Elephant, what big ears you have? Remember the fox's reply "All the better to hear you with!" However an elephant's ears aren't simply for hearing better, but also to cool down the animal in hot climates.

Did you know that elephants can become an excellent robber?! Elephant feet are covered in a padding that avoids slipping and uphold weight and therefore they can easily walk silently without making a noise!

Be gentle when talking to an elephant! Elephants are highly sensitive and caring. They express grief, compassion, and are very joyful.

All of us are either right handed or left handed and, similarly, elephants also have a tusk which they prefer one over another.

One thing you'd hate about elephants is how they shove mud all over themselves. Eww! But did you know that elephants do this to prevent burning from the sun? Yes, it acts as a natural sunscreen! So the next time your mom scolds you for playing with mud, you have an excuse!

It is certainly good news to find out that elephants live up to over 70 years old!

How about offering peanuts to an elephant? Bad idea. Elephants certainly do not like eating peanuts.

Someone is purring but it is not your cat! Perhaps it is an elephant! Elephants communicate with each other by making a noise like a cat's purr.

It is interesting to know that elephants have often been used during wars because of their intelligence. And next time there is a circus in your city, see if an elephant is in it. These gentle giants are easy to train and are used to perform!

Cows are not the only cows that live. Even a female elephant is called a cow and a male is called a bull! Guess what a baby elephant is called? That's right, a calf!

With their large bodies, it is hard to imagine an elephant swimming, but it does!
Elephants are great swimmers and what's more? They lift their trunks like a snorkel!

Did you know that elephants have a Day of the Dead like us?! In fact, whenever they pass by an elephant's dead body or a place where their loved ones have died, elephants stay still and silent for several minutes.

Hi there!
It's me, Jackie D. Fluffy!
I hope you like this book like I do.
What's the next animal you want to color??
Let me know by writing a review on

www.amazon.com

Sure! It will be fun and useful!
With much thanks and love,
Jackie D. Fluffy